A Guide to Executing Change for the Project Management Team

Participant Workbook

Wayne R. Davis

T0344958

Pfeiffer

A Wiley Imprint

www.pfeiffer.com

Published by Pfeiffer
An Imprint of Wiley
989 Market Street, San Francisco, CA 94103-1741
www.pfeiffer.com

For additional copies/bulk purchases of this book in the U.S. please contact 800-274-4434.

Pfeiffer books and products are available through most bookstores. To contact Pfeiffer directly call our Customer Care Department within the U.S. at 800-274-4434, outside the U.S. at 317-572-3985, fax 317-572-4002, or visit www.pfeiffer.com.

Pfeiffer also publishes its books in a variety of electronic formats. Some content that appears in print may not be available in electronic books.

Project Management Team: Participant Workbook ISBN: 978-0-470-40007-4

Acquiring Editor: Holly Allen
Marketing Manager: Tolu Babalola
Director of Development: Kathleen Dolan Davies
Developmental Editor: Susan Rachmeler
Production Editor: Michael Kay
Editor: Rebecca Taff
Assistant Editor: Marisa Kelley
Manufacturing Supervisor: Becky Morgan

Printed in the United States of America

Printing   10 9 8 7 6 5 4 3 2 1

Contents

1

Determine the Project Structure

FOLLOWING ARE THREE typical ways of organizing a change initiative project. Please review each chart and discuss the implications of each structure on the successful execution and outcomes of your change initiative.

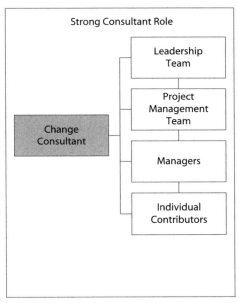

If you envision a model that is more suitable to your situation, please diagram it in the space below.

Project Structure and Organization Assessment

Referring to the charts on this and the previous page and considering your own situation, environment, and culture, complete the following assessment by reading each statement and checking the column for the role you believe serves the change initiative in the most beneficial way. Space is provided for you to enter and rate four additional criteria you believe should be considered. When you have completed the assessment, please sum each column by counting the number of check marks in each column and entering the totals in the spaces provided. Please check only **one** box for each statement.

Which role will provide the best results to

	Strong Leadership Role	Co-Sponsorship Role	Strong Consultant Role	Other Role
Mobilize people to act				
Make a compelling business case for change				
Keep the change initiative on course				
Ensure the change aligns to key business objectives				
Reinforce the need for change				
Set the priorities for successful execution				
Ensure integration of change initiatives with business goals				
Challenge the status quo				
Measure the progress and effectiveness of change				
Solve problems and make decisions				
Make the connection between the new behaviors and success				
Address chaos and complexity				
Ensure the development and delivery of essential training				
Create a value-based change model and roadmap				
Develop a communication strategy and plan				
Ensure change is localized and internalized				
Develop assessment instruments and evaluation tools				
Add four additional criteria:				
A.				
B.				
C.				
D.				
TOTAL				

Exercise Summary: Project Structure and Organization

As a group, you'll share your scores. When the facilitator has completed this portion of the exercise, enter the sum totals for all participants in the spaces provided below.

	Strong Leadership Role
	Strong Co-Sponsorship Role
	Strong Consultant Role
	Other Role

The facilitator will conduct an exercise to help determine the **strengths and weaknesses** of your selected role. Enter the results of the exercise in the appropriate spaces below. The higher scores are strengths and the lower scores weaknesses. Discuss how you will address and deal with the weaknesses.

Mobilize people to act		Solve problems and make decisions	
Make a compelling business case for change		Make the connection between the new behaviors and success	
Keep the change initiative on course		Address chaos and complexity	
Ensure the change aligns to key business objectives		Ensure the development and delivery of essential training	
Reinforce the need for change		Create a value-based change model and roadmap	
Set the priorities for successful execution		Develop a communication strategy and plan	
Ensure integration of change initiatives with business goals		Ensure change is localized and internalized	
Challenge the status quo		Develop assessment instruments and evaluation tools	
Measure the progress and effectiveness of change			

Following the determination of strengths and weaknesses, as a group, you'll discuss the following questions:

- What are the implications?
- How should these opportunities for development be dealt with?
- Who does what and by when?

Notes

_____

_____

_____

_____

_____

_____

_____

_____

_____

_____

_____

_____

_____

_____

_____

_____

_____

_____

_____

_____

_____

Determine the Project Resource Requirements

FOR EACH RESOURCE requirement listed below, check the box (we don't need; we need external resources; or we need internal resources) that reflects your view. Please clarify your choice by writing a brief comment in the space provided.

Resource Requirements Worksheet		
Resource Requirement	**External**	**Internal**
Change Consulting	Engage consultant(s) with appropriate change management experience to provide structure and process, and be a resource for advice, counsel, and direction.	Select key internal consultants who have previous experience with change management.
We don't need.	We need external resources.	We need internal resources.
Comment:		
Communication Consulting	Engage a communications consultant to distill and develop appropriate content for change communication and time, sequence and integrate program activities and messages	Rely on internal communications department.
We don't need.	We need external resources.	We need internal resources.
Comment:		

Training: Leadership Team, Change Team, Process Leaders, Contributors, Customers	Engage trainers to: Formulate a curriculum development plan; Construct learning objectives; Coordinate the training schedule; Deliver the training via appropriate platforms	Rely on internal training department to design, develop, and deliver training.	
We don't need.		We need external resources.		We need internal resources.	
Comment:			

Tools: Assessments, Special Software such as Project Management, etc.	Purchase assessment instruments and tools from external sources.	Relay on internal OD and project management departments for assessments and tools.	
We don't need.		We need external resources.		We need internal resources.	
Comment:			

Using the information from the worksheet on the preceding pages, please fill in the resource allocation information (time, rate, and money) for each relevant resource. You may also add additional resources if desired.

Requirement		Estimated Number of Days	Estimated Daily Rate	Estimated Amount
1.	**Change Consulting**			
1a.	Strategy development			
1b.	Project planning			
1c.	Deployment and execution			
2.	**Communication Consulting**			
2a.	Develop communication content			
2b.	Implement communication tracking system			
2c.	Integrate program activities and messages			
3.	**Training**			
3a.	Design and Development			
3b.	Delivery			
3c.	Leadership Team			
3d.	Change Team			
3e.	Process Leaders			
3f.	Individual Contributors			
3g.	Customers			
4.	**Assessments and Tools**			
4a.	Assessment: Change Style			
4b.	Assessment: Change Readiness			

Table title: **Estimated Project Budget Worksheet**

4c.	Assessment: Change Risk			
4d.	Assessment:			
4e.	Tools: Project Management			
4f.	Tools: Metrics and Indicators			
4g.	Tools:			
5.	**Other**			
		TOTAL ESTIMATED COST		

Notes

3

Identify Project Risks, Obstacles, and Barriers

FOR THIS ACTIVITY, you will complete the Change Risk Assessment, which provides an opportunity for you to determine the risk, obstacles, barriers, and complexity for change.

The seven risk components in this assessment include:

- Political
- Technology
- Cultural
- Financial
- Image
- Customer
- Know-How

The six obstacles and barriers components in this assessment include:

- Timeline
- Resources
- Commitment
- Resistance
- Two write-ins

The eight complexity components in this assessment include:

- Speed
- Disruption
- Direction
- Dimension
- Uncertainty
- Familiarization
- Dependency
- Political

Instructions

Each of the three portions of this assessment has its own instructions and scoring, which the facilitator will review with you. When working through this assessment, please answer every question. Do not leave any question unanswered.

Project Risks

Complete this portion of the assessment by reading each statement and checking the column that indicates your perception. *Note:* Please be aware that Columns 1 and 2 contain some reversed labels of "Yes" and "No."

Change Risk Assessment

Risks	1	2

Political	No	Yes
1. The political power factor is an issue in our organization and is exacerbated by top-down decision making and a command-and-control mentality.		
2. Counter-productive, and even bad or wrong decisions, are slow to be corrected.		
3. Reputation has it that in our company, advancement is by "who you know" not "what you know."		

Technology	No	Yes
4. With new projects, IT in our organization is generally over-optimistic.		
5. With new projects, IT in our organization has a reputation of schedule slide.		
6. With new projects, IT in our organization often complains about "feature creep."		

Cultural	Yes	No
7. Our people know our value system and generally follow it in conducting business.		
8. We're aware right away when there is a value shift that will reflect negatively on the organization.		
9. When confronted with heavy time demands, we insist our employees maintain a healthy work/life balance.		

Financial	No	Yes
10. Management's "pet" projects are rarely consolidated, reevaluated, or cancelled.		
11. Resource allocation is traditionally based on a "favorite son" lineup.		

Image	Yes	No
12. When consolidation or downsizing is required, we have a plan in place that assures people's dignity and self-worth.		
13. We do whatever it takes to maintain our "company of choice" image.		

Risks	1	2

Customer	Yes	No
14. We regularly invite customers to be members of our planning, product development, and cost-containment teams.		
15. We currently have a plan in place that will monitor the affects of this change initiative on our customers.		

Know-How	No	Yes
16. We tend to rely on our own expertise and are not convinced that third parties bring much value to the table.		
17. We encourage the opinions of others, but generally act on ideas put forth by the senior staff.		
18. Our workforce as a whole is very good at what they do, but they don't understand the business in the same way as the senior staff.		
Add the number of checks in each column and enter the totals here. <div align="right">TOTAL</div>		
Calculate the percentages in each column by dividing the total for each column by 18. <div align="right">**PERCENT***</div>		

*If the percentage of 2s is 20 percent or higher, that is an indicator of potential roadblocks occurring during the change process. Remember, all items checked in Column 2 are opportunities for improvement.

Obstacles and Barriers Assessment

Conduct this assessment by writing responses to the question posed in each category. Please add two additional obstacles and/or barriers and your response in the space provided below.

Timeline

How will you deal with compressed timelines?

Resources

How will you address the issue of an inadequate budget?

Commitment

How will you confront unenthusiastic commitment?

Resistance

How will you turn resistance to change into a positive force?

1.

2.

Complexity Assessment

Complete this assessment by reading each statement and circling the number in the scale box according to how you perceive the statement characterizes your situation.

Complexity and Risk of Change			
1. Speed of change. How fast will the change be?	We will fall behind.	We will keep up.	We will stay ahead.
	0 .... 25 .... 50 .... 75 100		
2. Disruption of change. How much chaos will it create?	Chaos will abound.	Some disruption	Little/no disruption
	0 .... 25 .... 50 .... 75 100		
3. Direction of change. How far out of our comfort zone?	Brand new road ahead	Familiar, some detours	Well-traveled road
	0 .... 25 .... 50 .... 75 100		
4. Dimension of change. How deep will the change go?	Will touch all	Will touch many	Will touch few
	0 .... 25 .... 50 .... 75 100		
5. Uncertainty of change. How good are we at changing?	We're not very good at change.	We've gone through similar change.	We've got a lot of experience.
	0 .... 25 .... 50 .... 75 100		
6. Uncharted water of change. How familiar are we with where we're headed?	We're in over our heads.	We can tread water and get our bearings.	We're good swimmers.
	0 .... 25 .... 50 .... 75 100		
7. Dependency factors. Do we have control of all of the parts?	We will depend heavily on others.	We have control of some but not all major parts.	Everything is entirely within our control.
	0 .... 25 .... 50 .... 75 100		
8. Political factors. Is everyone on board?	There are skeptics and doubters.	A lot of wait-and-see.	There is substantial buy-in.
	0 .... 25 .... 50 .... 75 100		

Complexity of Change

Record the value (0, 25, 50, 75, 100) you gave for each statement in the appropriate spaces below.

1	
2	
3	
4	
5	
6	
7	
8	

Add the numbers in the second column and enter the grand total here.

Discussion

What single component or factor in the assessment do you feel is the most impacting on your organization?

Why?

What additional components of complexity and risk do you feel should be included for your organization?

Notes

_____

_____

_____

_____

_____

_____

_____

_____

_____

_____

_____

_____

_____

_____

_____

_____

_____

_____

_____

4

Determine Information Needs

COMPLETE THIS EXERCISE by providing the input required to complete each row and column. The legend for the value code is at the bottom of the worksheet. For "Source," check whether the information will be obtained internally or externally. For acquisition cost, insert the dollar amount necessary to obtain the information. Add any other categories or subjects you feel are needed on the supplemental sheet on page 25.

Information Needs Worksheet

Category/Subject	Value Code*	Source		Acquisition Cost	When Needed
		Internal	**External**		
Business					
Financial information					
Statistical data					
Technical					
Applications (software)					
Platforms (hardware)					
Markets					
Served: current, emerging					
Un-served: current, emerging					
Suppliers					
Customers					
Competitors					
Policy					
Code of conduct					
Ethical standards					
Legal					
Change plan review					
Regulations review					
Data					
Surveys and feedback					
Employee census data					
Research					
Benchmarks					
Best practices					
Advisory					
Subject-matter experts					
Trusted advisors					
TOTAL ESTIMATED COST				$	

*Legend:

Code	*Value*
C	*Critical*
H	*Highly Valuable*
G	*Good to Have*

Information Needs Supplemental Worksheet

Category/Subject	Value Code*	Source		Acquisition Cost	When Needed
		Internal	External		
TOTAL ESTIMATED COST				$	

*Legend:

Code	Value
C	Critical
H	Highly Valuable
G	Good to Have

Notes

_____

_____

_____

_____

_____

_____

_____

_____

_____

_____

_____

_____

_____

_____

_____

_____

_____

_____

_____

_____

5

Build a Project Calendar with Events and a Timeline

COMPLETE THE EXERCISE by indicating the date or duration you perceive the event should take place. See the example below for marking the calendar. In your calendar, under each major event, you can insert detailed related sub-tasks. Add any additional events that you deem necessary on the calendar on page 29.

Examples													
Event		**Timeline**											
	Time Periods >	1	2	3	4	5	6	7	8	9	10	11	12
Time-specific example			x										
Duration example				●—————————————●									

Project Calendar												
Event	**Timeline**											
Time Periods >	1	2	3	4	5	6	7	8	9	10	11	12
Project Announcement												
Change Management Strategy and Plan												
Final Project Schedule												
Communication Strategy and Plan												
Measurement Strategy and Plan												

Event		Timeline											
	Time Periods >	1	2	3	4	5	6	7	8	9	10	11	12
Evaluation Strategy and Plan													
Additional Items													

Notes

6

Identify Measures and Indicators

IN THIS EXERCISE, you will develop measurements and indicators that:

- Create a direct link between performance and goals
- Define a common language to communicate measurement and actions
- Ensure no important aspect is missed
- Give control over business direction and results
- Create clear communication of what goals and metrics are important
- Allow for preventive actions and timely resolution

To complete this activity, put a check in the zone column (red, yellow, or green) that represents your perception of your organization's ability to track each measure/indicator. At the bottom of the worksheet, add four additional measures or indicators you feel are important for you to track. Some examples are provided after the worksheet.

Measurement and Indicator Worksheet

Measure/Indicator	Zone (Check One)		
	Red (Next to Impossible)	Yellow (This Will Be a Struggle)	Green (We Can Do This)
New skills areas have been identified and trained.			
Supporting structures to prevent reversion are in place.			
New practices and processes are implemented and working.			
Alignment with the new business model is evident.			
Managers and supervisors are providing a clarity of mission.			
Customers are commenting positively on the new changes.			
People are using the new language and "code words."			
Employees have made the connection between the new behaviors and success.			
1.			
2.			
3.			
4.			
Total Number of Check Marks			

Examples

Here are some additional ideas for measurement. For example, if the organization is a **call center**, it would necessarily be concerned about:

Reliability

- Promise to do something by a certain time, and do it
- Perform the service right the first time
- Make it a "wow" experience

Responsiveness

- Tell customers exactly when services will be performed
- Give prompt service to customers
- Always be willing to support and help customers

Assurance

- Instill confidence in customers
- Be patient and courteous
- Have the knowledge to answer customer questions

Empathy

- Give customers individual attention
- Understand their specific needs, put yourself in their shoes
- Have customers' best interests at heart

If the change initiative focuses on **operational excellence**, the metrics could be:

Accuracy Metrics

- Picking error rate
- Inventory variance
- Shipment reject rate

Productivity Metrics

- Receiving turnaround
- Shipment confirmations
- Direct productivity
- Four-walls productivity

Employee Management Metrics

- Absentee rate
- Overtime labor rate

Site Metrics

- Warehouse environment
- Stale paper report

Compliance and Quality Metrics

- DOT violations
- Q+ recognition

As time permits, you may find it helpful to discuss the following list of terms and descriptive characteristics and further define these terms within your own context.

How do we measure and track…?	Descriptive Characteristics
Efficiency	Is the measure of the relationship of outputs to inputs and usually expressed as a ratio, for example, unit cost per output, labor productivity, cycle time, etc.
Effectiveness	Is the measure of output conformance to specified characteristics, for example, number of transactions competed by target time, number of defect-free products, etc.
Quality	Is a characteristic or standard measure of excellence measured by the degree to which it meets that standard.
Service delivery	Is measuring the things that customers care about, for example, being able to speak to a real person rather than voice mail, etc.
Idea generation	Is creativity and innovation shown through qualitative indicators of the rate of introduction of managerial or technological innovations into the work process.
Productivity	Is output characterized by a discrete definition of the service you perform or the product you make.
Performance	Is data collected to determine how well you are doing, for example, the percentage of defective items returned, the number of customer complaints, or the length of time taken to complete a transaction, etc.

Notes